THE LONG AND DARING JOURNEY
~ Basic Version for the General Public ~

By:

Shenna McLaughlin

Edited By:
G.R.Fitch

Proof Read & Edited By:
Dixie Fitch
Maria C. Cortes
&
Beth McLaughlin

Technical Sturgeon Details,
Assistance, & Additional Illustrations
By:
G.R.Fitch

This book is formatted in large type so that it can be easily shown while being read.

THE LONG AND DARING JOURNEY

This story was inspired by the Sturgeon Presentation
By G.R.Fitch.
Presented to the 3rd Grade Class of U.V.C.S. on
May 9th 2008

"Sturgy the Sturgeon"

THE LONG AND DARING JOURNEY

CONTENTS:

THE LONG AND DARING JOURNEY

CHAPTER 1

THE JOURNEY BEGINS

"Hi! My name is Sally, Sally the Sturgeon.

My Grandma just passed away leaving behind thousands of eggs. I could hardly believe it!

She has laid eggs a lot of times. In fact, this would have been her 23rd time."

I know, it's amazing huh?

I could hardly believe it, but before she left us she told us a story, a story passed down from all grandmothers before her, and the story of the long and daring journey."

"I was just about to go on a journey of my own but I still have a little bit of time left so I think I'll tell you the story."

It all started a long time ago, about 20,000 years in the past. A long, long time ago…

"I'm ready, I'm ready!" Sturgy the Sturgeon sang as she swam over the sand.

She was 17 years old now and had thousands of babies coming. She swam around her seaweed home for the last time before giving her most favorite possessions away.

Her favorite possessions were first of all, a fin written letter by her mother before her that said:

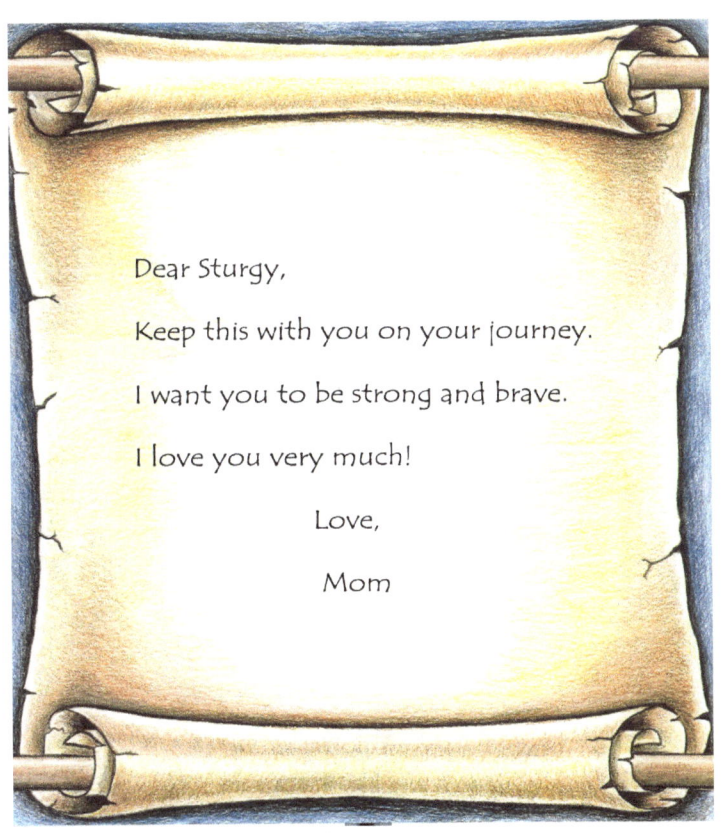

Dear Sturgy,

Keep this with you on your journey.

I want you to be strong and brave.

I love you very much!

Love,

Mom

The other thing was 200 clams from her mother for the journey.

Sturgy slipped these in her pack and swam to meet the other fish who were waiting to start their own migration journey.

"We're off!" sang the head fish, and they swam North up the river.

THE LONG AND DARING JOURNEY

CHAPTER 2

A NEW FOUND FRIEND

Sturgy had been swimming along, by herself, in the line of fish for hours and was getting rather lonely. So, she decided that she would swim up the line and try to find a friend.

She swam up to a fish in front of her and said,

"Hi! I'm Sturgy the White Sturgeon. Who are you?"

"Carl," was his gruff answer.

"Oh!" Sturgy said in surprise as she watched Carl, the Shad, swim away.

(What went wrong) She thought;

(I just wanted to be friends. I guess I'll try the next one)

So, she tried again.

"Hi, I'm Sturgy the White Sturgeon. Who are you?"

No response.

Although Sturgy tried very hard, she got the same results. She tried again and again, but the same thing happened every time.

No response.

Sturgy was on her fifth try and was about to give up when someone actually acknowledged her, nicely.

"Hi!" The other fish responded,

"I'm Stephanie the Sturgeon."

"Oh!" said Sturgy in surprise,

"What kind of Sturgeon?"

"A White Sturgeon." Stephanie answered promptly.

"Oh, Wow, me too!" exclaimed Sturgy.

"Oh, that's great! Maybe, just maybe we could swim together." replied Stephanie.

"But before we do, may I ask you a question?" asked Sturgy.

"Sure." said Stephanie.

"Well, why are all the other fish so mean?" she asked.

"Oh, that's easy," said Stephanie.

"What is!" exclaimed Sturgy.

"Well." Stephanie said taking her time.

"They don't like us White Sturgeon because we're so smart and 1st class."

"Ohhhh, is that all?" said Sturgy.

"Yep." replied Stephanie.

"Wow!" exclaimed Sturgy and continued,

"Well, anyway shouldn't we be going?"

"Yes, we should get going." replied Stephanie and Sturgy said,

"Then let's go!"

And off they went charging ahead to the group that was a few feet ahead of them, so it seemed.

They didn't know it but the group of fish were actually swimming away from them and were a few miles ahead by now.

THE LONG AND DARING JOURNEY

CHAPTER 3

A NEW ADVENTURE

The two new friends swam as fast as they could but the group was way in front of them.

"Geez, they're going really fast." said Sturgy.

"Ya." agreed Stephanie.

"I thought they were only a few feet away but this looks like a couple of miles," she continued.

"I agree." said Sturgy.

"But anyway, I think we should hurry up if we're going to catch up with them." Sturgy told Stephanie.

"Okay," said Stephanie.

"HEY!"

"HEY, you guys wait up," yelled both Sturgy and Stephanie.

The group of fish turned their heads at the same time and smiled meanly. Then with a burst of speed they rounded a corner with a large rock.

A thought suddenly struck Sturgy. (Are they trying to swim away from us? I better not tell Stephanie because she'll panic.)

"Well, we better swim a bit faster," Sturgy told Stephanie.

"Ya, I agree," Stephanie said.

"Race you to them," she ended.

The two Sturgeon charged up to the rock.

No fish.

Puzzled, they swam around the rock.

Still no sign of them.

"Where have they gone?" asked Sturgy, now very alarmed herself.

"I, I, I don't know, they left us. They knew we were a better species of fish and they just deserted us," stammered Stephanie.

"Ya, they must have had a really bad reputation of us," said Sturgy with anger in her voice.

"Hold on there!" Stephanie said.

"We can be the first 2 fish to make it to the spawning grounds by ourselves, without any help."

"I still think they shouldn't have left us here and we should go back." Sturgy said in a disagreeable way.

"Oh, come on, please?" pleaded Stephanie.

"Oh, all right, fine. Maybe this will be an adventure after all," said Sturgy with new hope.

They swam and swam, fin in fin, for hours and hours. They were getting very tired when Stephanie said,

"Hey, I think the spawning grounds are that way!"

She pointed a fin north from where they rested.

"All right, let's go that way," Sturgy agreed.

They took off down a swift channel thinking of adventures that they would have.

They were so caught up in their thoughts that they didn't even notice when the group of missing fish came out in front of them.

The fish emerged from a secret cave and swam in the other direction.

THE LONG AND DARING JOURNEY

CHAPTER 4

THE HOTEL

Sturgy and Stephanie had been swimming for an hour or so when Sturgy spotted a town in the distance.

"Hey, look!" exclaimed Sturgy excitedly.

"There must be a town ahead," said Stephanie sharing Sturgys excitement.

"Let's go there, maybe they have a hotel, or restaurant where we can spend the night," said Stephanie and continued.

"We can get up in the morning and have an early breakfast. We can then find the current and take that until we reach the river channel. From there we will take the route up the river." She continued on.

"We will have to take the dangerous route of the dinosaur eating grounds. Then, we will have to take the north route that is close to what is called the "Arctic." We will have to be on the lookout for seals and fishing hooks. Then, if we continue going on that route, it will lead us to the spawning grounds," said Stephanie all in one breath.

"That is if we find a motel," said Sturgy sarcastically.

Stephanie sighed, "That's true, so we better go find out."

"Race you there."

With a swoosh of bubbles Stephanie had gotten a head start.

"Hey, wait a sec!" shouted Sturgy trying to catch up.

But Stephanie was paying no attention to her. She quickly crossed the border of the town and won the race.

After a minute, or two, Sturgy caught up to her breathing heavily.

"I won!" said Stephanie giggling at Sturgys tired face.

"Ya," said Sturgy getting her energy back and said with a tired voice.

"Good job."

"Thanks!" said Stephanie and continued.

"Well, why don't we look for a hotel?"

"Okay," agreed Sturgy.

"I'll swim down this lane and you go down that one over there. We will meet up after we've reached the end and see what luck we've had." Sturgy directed.

"Okay, bye-bye," said Stephanie swimming down her lane.

"Okay, see ya," called out Sturgy.

As Sturgy swam down her lane she noticed how nice the town was. It had about three restaurants, a gill trimmer shop, a mall, a souvenir shop, and a hotel.

(Great.) Thought Sturgy.

So, she swam a bit faster back to find Stephanie, which she shortly did.

"Stephanie, Stephanie," cried out Sturgy.

"I found a hotel. Let's go get reservations. Come on!" said Sturgy eagerly pulling on Stephanie's fin.

"Okay," said Stephanie as she was being pulled along by Sturgy.

Much to the surprise of Sturgy and Stephanie the hotel was big and beautiful. It was four stories high and six rooms across. It was an orange coral building with blue trim around the windows and doors, and across the top of the building it said in big, bold, blue letters:

The Swishy Fishy

Hotel

"Wow!" yelled Sturgy with excitement.

"Let's go in." She continued as she charged towards the door.

"Hold on a sec!" cried Stephanie as Sturgy immediately stopped.

"I have a plan," Stephanie said.

"Why don't we go in and look at some brochures for this river and the next. They should have maps, and we can find out where we can go from here, and if there are any hotels closer to where we are going that are cheaper." finished Stephanie.

"That's a good plan," said Sturgy.

"Let's do that."

"All right." Said Stephanie happily.

"Follow me." She said as she led Sturgy and herself through the door.

THE LONG AND DARING JOURNEY

CHAPTER 5

MR. CRAWDAD

"Welcome!" greeted Mr. Crawdad at the front counter.

"Would you like to stay at our hotel?" he asked with excitement in his voice.

"Um, actually we were looking for brochures," Stephanie answered.

"Oh, uh, they're in the breakfast room. Just over there, first door on the left." he said pointing his claw towards an open doorway.

"Thank you," Sturgy and Stephanie said together.

They swam over and through the open doorway. There was fresh seaweed carpet and mussel shell windows. The walls were painted a pearl color, probably with pearl paint.

(This is quite a place.) Thought Sturgy.

"All right, here they are," said Stephanie swimming up to a bookshelf like stand made of tree limbs that was filled with brochures.

Sturgy selected a blue brochure with the words:

~ *Fishy, Fishy, Food Hotel* ~ across the front of it.

(That sounds too much like a restaurant.) Thought Sturgy.

She picked out another one. On it was a picture of an empty giant clam with windows and doors and on one corner it said:

"The most comfortable seaweed beds ever!"
"Not too Clamy!"
"It smells bad as well!"

She picked up another brochure. It had a picture of Sandy Bar Park.

(Nope.) Thought Sturgy. I'm not sleeping in any park.

Stephanie and she looked at a few more brochures with the same results. Nothing seemed as good as this hotel.

Sturgy looked over at Stephanie and she seemed to be having the same feeling.

"So, I guess it's here," said Sturgy trying to sound disappointed, even though she really wanted to stay here.

"Well, I guess you're right," agreed Stephanie.
"Let's go get our reservations."

They swam over to the counter where Mr. Crawdad was and he looked upset.
"Leaving all ready?" he said sounding very upset.
"Oh, no, actually we're going to stay." said Stephanie.
Mr. Crawdads face lit up.
"You're staying?"
"Great!" He exclaimed.
"I can assign you two to room eleven on the second floor, a very nice room," he said.
"Thank you," said Stephanie.
"This will only be for today, tonight, and until eleven o'clock tomorrow," informed Sturgy.
"Okay, very good," responded Mr. Crawdad.
"That will be 3 clams a fish," he told them.
"Okay!" said Sturgy and Stephanie at the same time.

They eagerly handed Mr. Crawdad the clams and in exchange he gave them the keys to their room.
"Thank you," said Sturgy and Stephanie together.

They swam up the stairway to room eleven and once there they unlocked the door and went in.

The room was large with a T.V., dresser, closet, restroom, and two twin beds. It also had a tiny table with four chairs and finally a big window overlooking the town below.

"Wow!" said Stephanie.

"This place is great!"

"Ya," said Sturgy as she put her few possessions in the closet.

Grrrr………went something in the room.

Sturgy gasped and Stephanie giggled.

"I guess I'm just a tad bit hungry," Stephanie said stifling another giggle.

"Only a tad bit?" questioned Sturgy.

"You sound like you haven't eaten in a hundred years," she exclaimed.

"Well, it does feel that way." Said Stephanie honestly.

"Well then, what are we waiting for?" said Sturgy.

"Let's go see what this place has to offer for dinner."

So, Sturgy and Stephanie swam out the door and down the hall. They were so pleased when they picked up the scent of fresh salmon eggs with their whiskers that they swam even faster.

But as they swam a knocking sound came from the other side of the wall.

They didn't hear it, but they should have.

They definitely should have.

THE LONG AND DARING JOURNEY

CHAPTER 6

THE NOTE & THE OTHER GIRLS

After dinner they swam back to their room.

"Ahhhh," said Stephanie as she swam onto her bed.

"I'm not hungry any more."

She had just finished eating a dinner of salmon eggs, mussel meat, shrimp juice, and salmon turnover cake.

"I know how you feel," said Sturgy.

"I'm sooooo stuffed."

They laid there happy for a minute or so until they heard a knocking noise. They looked at the door just as an envelope slid under it.

"Oh my gosh," said Stephanie as she picked up the envelope, opened it, and pulled out a piece of paper. She unfolded the paper and read it aloud.

In neat handwriting the note said:

"Welcome!

Come over to room 12

at once!"

Sturgy and Stephanie looked at each other and shrugged before they swam out the door and over to room twelve. Once there they knocked on the door with apprehension and anticipation.

Much to their surprise three Sturgeon, that looked about 16 or 17 years old, opened the door.

"Hi!" One of them greeted.

"My name is Annie," she said.

"My name is Patty," said another.

And finally.

"My name is Cathy," said the last one with a little smile.

"It's nice to meet you," she said.

"It's nice to meet you too," said Sturgy smiling.

"But tell me, why did you ask us to come over?" she said.

"Well!" said Patty.

"Come in and we'll tell you the whole story."

Stephanie and Sturgy went into the girls room and noticed it was a lot like theirs.

They all sat on the comfortable furniture and began their talk.

"Annie can tell you," said Cathy generously.

"Thank you," said Annie;

"But let me begin with;"

"We were once three Sturgeon of a group of 300 other fish. When they figured out that we were White Sturgeon they ditched us. We swam for days and finally found this place."

"We have lived here ever since."

"Oh, I'm sorry," said Stephanie;

" It must have been rather boring."

"Actually, it wasn't, but it was very, very hard work," Annie said.

"Hard work?" asked Sturgy.

"What do you mean?"

"Well, we have made something very wonderful that we would like to show you," said Cathy.

"Really?" asked Stephanie.

"What is it?" Sturgy then asked.

"Oh, it's a surprise," responded Patty

"But if you come back here tomorrow at 5:00 in the morning we will show it to you," added Annie.

"Oh!" exclaimed Sturgy.

"Well, I'm going to bed right now. The faster you go to bed, the faster morning comes and the faster we get to see the surprise," said Sturgy quickly and with excitement.

"Then let's go to sleep," said Stephanie.

"Bye, bye." They said as they left.

"Bye, bye," said the three Sturgeon.

Sturgy and Stephanie just sat in their beds. Neither of them could sleep.

"I wonder what the surprise is," said Stephanie.

"Maybe it's a blue fishamobile," guessed Sturgy.

"Or a beautiful pink coral necklace," added Stephanie.

"Or a mechanical starfish," said Sturgy.

"Or a supply of Salmon eggs to last us a lifetime," said Stephanie with a glimmer of hope in her eyes.

"Or a……"

But before Sturgy could finish her head drooped onto her pillow and she fell into a very deep sleep.

THE LONG AND DARING JOURNEY

CHAPTER 7

ANOTHER ADVENTURE

The morning soon came.

Sturgy woke up and looked at the clock and it was 4:30. She thought that was enough time to get up, tidy up the hotel room, brush her Scutes, and head over to room 12 to meet the other Sturgeon.

Sturgy gently shook Stephanie awake.

"Huh, what time is it?" Stephanie mumbled.

"It's 4:31, and we can see the surprise in 29 minutes," said Sturgy.

Immediately Stephanie was out of bed and brushing her Scutes.

"I can't wait," said Stephanie setting down the brush and racing to make her bed.

"What time is it now?" she asked.

"4:36," answered Sturgy as she swam as fast as she could to the closet and took her things out and set them on the bed. She couldn't wait for 5:00 either.

"I've finished making my bed, I've brushed my Scutes, and it's still not five o'clock," complained Stephanie.

"I know how you feel. I've done all of those things too and it's only 4:40," sighed Sturgy.

"Twenty more minutes," complained Stephanie.

"There's only one more thing to do that we haven't already done,"
said Sturgy.

"What?" asked Stephanie.

"We could explore the big beautiful building on the lane that you saw," replied Sturgy as she continued;
"Remember how you just couldn't stop talking about it at dinner last night."

"Oh, of course, I remember now," replied Stephanie.

"But why don't we just take a peek at it and see if you like it. And, if you do then we can explore it thoroughly later if you want to," asked Stephanie.

"Okay," agreed Sturgy.

"Then lets go!" cried out Stephanie;
"We don't want to waste any more time, we're down to only 18 minutes until 5:00," she said as she and Sturgy swam out of the door.

They swam down the hall, down the stairs, across the lobby, and out the front door of the hotel. They swam up the first lane and down the second lane until they saw it.

It was a beautiful building made out of "Floating Bark" as the fish called it. It was painted white and had beautiful stained glass windows. There was even a tower with a pointed roof and a bell hanging from inside it that you could see from a small opening.

"It's just beautiful," said Sturgy.

"Isn't it?" said Stephanie.

"Yes." agreed Sturgy.

"I would love to come here again," she said.

"Great!" cried out Stephanie.

"Well it's 4:55 and we better get back to the hotel."

"Okay," said Sturgy.

"Let's just hope your watch isn't off time," she said with a giggle.

"Let's hurry back to the hotel just in case it is," she said as she giggled again.

The two of them swam back to the hotel as fast as they could.

As they went through the doors the hand on the clock moved to 4:56. They swam up the stairs and it moved to 4:57. As they stepped into the hall it turned to 4:58.

Time was flying by with their anticipation.

They swam down the hall and it ticked to 4:59 and then as they knocked on the door of room 12 the clock struck 5:00.

Patty opened up the door.

"Welcome, come in," she said happily.

"Let me go get my sisters and then we can show you the surprise."

Patty turned around and went into the other room. She came back with Annie and Cathy who looked very tired. Cathy looked at her coral watch.

"You came just on time," she remarked.

"Ya, we were up at four-thirty trying to find things to do." Said Stephanie with a dramatic pause.

"Wow!" exclaimed Annie.

"Four-thirty!" she said.

"Uh-huh," said Sturgy

"But enough talking, I really, really want to find out what that surprise is," she said being a wee-bit bossy.

Patty laughed.

"All right," she said.

"Let's go!"

THE LONG AND DARING JOURNEY

The small group of Sturgeon turned around, swam out of the door and down the hall. They swam out of the hall, down the stairs, through the doors, and off the hotel grounds.

They swam in the direction that Stephanie and Sturgy had come when they entered the town. They all swam together for about five more minutes until they reached a patch of seaweed bushes.
Patty swam over to the bushes.
" All right, look over this way," she said as she pulled one of the bushes aside.
Sturgy couldn't believe her eyes.

Annie, Cathy, and Patty giggled at the astonished face of Sturgy. "What is it?" Sturgy asked.

THE LONG AND DARING JOURNEY

CHAPTER 8

THE FANCY BUILDIING

Before her eyes was a channel that stretched out at least five miles. It was farther than she could see.

"It's a channel, or a short cut, to the spawning grounds." Cathy said.

"If you didn't take this short cut you would have to swim 500 miles." remarked Annie.

"My goodness!" exclaimed Sturgy.

"Who's been on it before?" she asked.

"Oh, me, my sisters, you, and Stephanie are the first and only ones to know about it, let alone use it." Annie answered.

"WOW!" exclaimed Sturgy.

"I have a question now," said Stephanie with her fin raised.

"When are we going to use it?"

"Oh, I don't know," answered Cathy.

"When do you two leave the hotel?" She asked.

"Oh we were going to leave at 11:00 but if you want us to leave sooner…"

Patty cut her off and said,

"Oh no, 11:00 is fine."

"Perfect!" exclaimed Annie.

"Yes, perfect," echoed Cathy as she continued,

"Because then we can be at the spawning grounds around 2:00 and each find our perfect spots.

"Okay," said Stephanie.

"Well, we've better get going," said Sturgy.

"All right, you two get going," agreed Annie.

"Bye!" yelled Sturgy and Stephanie waving their fins as they swam away and straight to their room to make plans before they left.

"Okay." said Sturgy as she laid on her bed;

"I have an idea of how we could do things, if you would like to hear it."

"Okay." Stephanie said eagerly.

"All right, here it goes." said Sturgy

"We could go down and get some breakfast first, then from there we can go to that fancy building, be done at 10:45 and come back here. We could get our stuff, check out, and go to the secret channel."

"Great idea!" exclaimed Stephanie.

"So, what's the first on the list? It's go to the fancy building?" She asked.

"No, it's going to breakfast," said Sturgy.

"No, isn't it checking out, or going to the channel. No, no, it's….." Stephanie said as she argued with herself.

"Why don't I just say the list over again?" suggested Sturgy.
"Fine." agreed Stephanie.
"Okay." said Sturgy as she repeated the list.

"1.) Breakfast.

2.) Fancy Building.

3.) Get Stuff.

4.) Check out.

5.) Go to Channel.

Done"

"Okay." said Stephanie.
"I think I got it."
"Okay." said Sturgy.
"Let's go down to breakfast."

Stephanie followed Sturgy out of the door and headed with her down the hall, and down the stairs, to the breakfast room.

At breakfast, Sturgy chewed slowly on a bite of delicious worm pancake. She was thinking of Mr. Crawdad, the owner of the hotel. He seemed unusually sad and kind of upset. Sturgy thought about how he seemed sad when Stephanie said they might leave, and how he seemed happy when they said they were going to stay.

Sturgy began to think to herself,

(Maybe his business is bad with the hotel) She thought.

(Or maybe………)

Stephanie gave her a playful slap on the cheek.

"Hello, anybody home?" she teased.

Sturgy smiled and said, "I was just thinking."

"About what?" asked Stephanie

"Oh, well, have you noticed what I have noticed about Mr. Crawdad?" Sturgy asked seriously.

Stephanie who had been playing with her food looked up and said,

"You mean how sad he is?" she asked.

"Ya, I think…." but Sturgy stopped short and said,

"Oh, here comes the waitress."

"Are you done with those worm pancakes miss?" She asked Sturgy with an English accent.

"Oh, yes." said Sturgy and continued.

"Can I ask you a question?"

The waitress smiled sweetly and said nicely,

"Of course you may dear."

"Okay, why is Mr. Crawdad always so sad?" Sturgy asked.

Just then the nice and easy smile of the waitress turned into a very mad scowl. She picked up Sturgys' worm pancakes and swam away.

"Oh!" exclaimed Sturgy in surprise.

"Um, why don't we finish our salmon egg juice and head to the fancy building." said Stephanie modestly.

"Right." said Sturgy before she gulped down her juice and got out of her chair.

Stephanie did the same and together they swam out of the front door of the hotel without even looking to see if Mr. Crawdad was there.

They swam up the first lane and down the second lane until they saw the fancy building. It was wonderful and beautiful so they both thought.

"Why don't we just go inside?" asked Stephanie.

"Uh, Okay," said Sturgy.

They swam through the big double doors and found themselves in a gigantic hall. They saw more big doors and swam over to them. Sturgy raised her fin and knocked.

A medium sized Trout answered her knock and opened the door.

"Hello." said Stephanie nervously.

"I'm sorry if we're intruding. It was my idea to knock and I will take the blame." She rambled on…

"It is such a beautiful building and we just had to check it out…."

She stopped when she saw a smile on the face of the Trout.

"It is fine," he said in a nice voice.

"I am Reverend Trout and this is a church open to all Fish."

he said with a smile.
  "You are both very welcome here.
  Please, come on in and follow me, I will show you around."

He led them through a room filled with beautiful things like shiny brown pews, stained glass windows, and a small stage with a podium on it.

Then he took them through some double doors and into a huge seagrass filled lawn with a pretty white fence around it.

From there he led them out a matching white gate with a river rock path leading to a small boulder with a door, window, and a roof upon it.

Sturgy and Stephanie were very amazed and delighted with all the beautiful things they saw.

(He must have carved it out himself and made it his home) Thought Stephanie as he led them down the path.

Reverend Trout went to the door, opened it, and went inside followed by Stephanie and Sturgy.

As they went in he gestured to them to rest on his beautiful velvet couch.

As they did he went into the kitchen and came back just seconds later with three tall glasses of shrimpade with ice floating on the top.

The Reverend sat down in his own chair with a loud, Ahhhh

He leaned forward and passed out the refreshments to the girls before looking at them and began to talk.

"Well now, what brings you girls here," he said.

Sturgy began.

"It's a very long story," she said

"And we don't have very much time," finished Stephanie

So, since they didn't have much time, they only spent half an hour more talking and having a tour of the church.

They thanked Reverend Trout for the tour, talking with them, and being so kind, and left the church.

They quickly headed back to the hotel.

THE LONG AND DARING JOURNEY

CHAPTER 9

THE STORY OF MR. CRAWDAD

Once back at the hotel they headed straight to their room and got their things. They left the room and went down the hall, down the stairs, and into the lobby for the last time.

When they got to the check out counter, they found Mr. Crawdad as sad as ever. They gave him their keys and he checked them out, his frown barely budging.

Stephanie's curiosity was just about to get the better of her. She tried to gulp down the words on the edge of her tongue, but accidentally blurted them out;

"Mr. Crawdad." she began.

"Why are you always so sad?"

In shock Stephanie quickly put her fins up to her mouth. She was horrified that she had actually said the words. She threw a guilty look over at Sturgy, but Sturgy didn't look mad at all. Instead, she looked interested to hear Mr. Crawdads answer.

Stephanie quickly turned her attention to Mr. Crawdad. He looked shocked too, but soon recovered. He looked at Stephanie and Sturgy straight in the eyes and said;

"It doesn't matter, you probably wouldn't care anyway."

Sturgy gasped and said,

"Of course we would, we want to help you in anyway we can." she explained.

The old crawdads face softened and there upon it was a smile.

Sturgy and Stephanie listened intently as he began.

"Well, last month my wife died very suddenly." He choked out the words.

"Then a few weeks later my children ran away. They didn't take anything precious with them just a few blankets and some food."

"Since then the police Bass have been looking for them but they can't find them."

"I have been very sad and no one likes it. They see my sad face and leave almost right away, this makes me very upset." Mr. Crawdad finished.

"Oh." said Stephanie,

"We're very sorry."

The crawdads grin faded.

"I told you there was nothing you could do." he said again.

"No!" exclaimed Sturgy.

"There might be something that we can do," she said thoughtfully.

"What?" asked Mr. Crawdad and continued to say,

"Are ya going to solve the mystery?"

"We just might," said Sturgy.

"Mr. Crawdad we're going to the spawning grounds right now but if we could come back here in about two weeks we might be able to solve your mystery," said Sturgy giving Stephanie a sideways glance and a wink.

Stephanie nodded and Sturgy turned back to Mr. Crawdad awaiting his answer.

"Yes, that would be fine." He said with excitement.

"But now I must say goodbye because I need to go and check on the baked seaweed that I will be serving for lunch." he said with a smile and a nod.

"And we need to get to the spawning grounds," said Sturgy.

They waved goodbye then turned and swam out the door.

THE LONG AND DARING JOURNEY

CHAPTER 10

THE EEL ATTACK

After Sturgy and Stephanie had talked to Mr. Crawdad, they swam directly to the secret channel where Annie, Patty, and Cathy were anxiously waiting for them.

"Wow!" said Sturgy.
"So we're the first ones to go in this channel?" she asked.
"Yes!" said Patty,
"We are."
Annie looked at Sturgy and Stephanie hopefully.
"Are you ready?" she asked.
"Yes!" shouted Sturgy and Stephanie together.
Annie and her sisters faces lit up.

"Great, then let's get going," Annie said.

"Wonderful!" said Cathy.

"Well, let's go!" said Patty taking the lead.

"Forward swim," she said.

Sturgy turned around and thought she saw a flash in the bushes on the other side of the channel but wasn't sure. She suddenly forgot about it because at that moment Patty, Cathy, Annie, and Stephanie started swimming away. So, she had to go in a hurry to catch up.

"Wow." I'm tired complained Cathy.
"Me too." said Annie.
"Me three." said Patty,
"Lets stop and rest over there in that clearing."

So, the five tired Sturgeon swam over to the clearing for a rest and
as Sturgy nestled down in the clearing she saw a familiar flashing in the distance. She squinted her eyes and saw that it wasn't flashing at all. It
was lamprey eels.

Sturgeon fear lamprey eels because they eat Sturgeon. Not only that, but the death they give is terrible. They just start eating the Sturgeon, not killing them at first. They make tunnels in the Sturgeon with their razor sharp teeth and slimy bodies and eat them up. It is very dreadful.

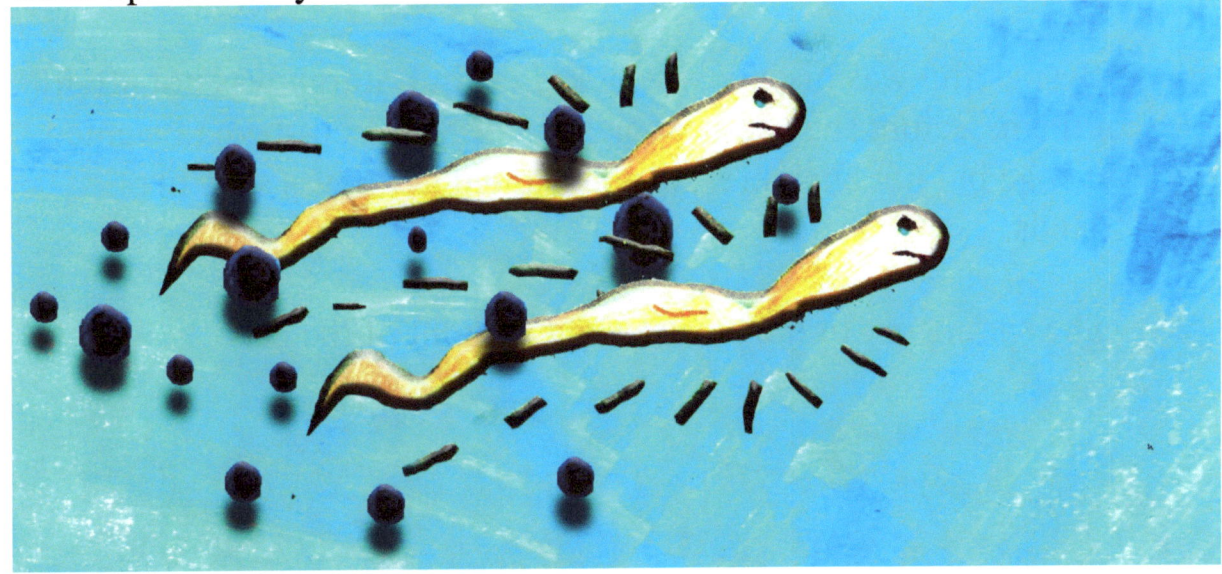

Sturgy gasped.
"Quick!" she said pushing the others,
"Lamprey eels!"

They all gasped and dove into the bushes.

Sturgy did the same, but she dove into a place where she could see out to the channel through the bushes.

Along came the eels with evil smiles on their faces.
"Hey!" cried out one with a snarling tone.
"Where did they go?" he said.

The eel didn't know Sturgy saw him and recognized him. He was Leone, the Lamprey Eel, that was known for his violence and cruelty.
But Sturgy knew him for a different reason. Leone was her worst enemy because he had eaten her mother and father.

Beside him was his evil sidekick, Lee, but Sturgy was not afraid of them. Before she had become a nicer Sturgeon she had wanted revenge but not anymore. All she wanted to do was save her friends.

She sprang out of the bushes right in front of the eels.

"Hey you little slimy monsters." she said while making a mean face.

She had to make them chase her, but how?

Sturgy thought fast.

(I've got it.) She thought.

(I'll make them chase me away.)

So she yelled out at them.

"You sure aren't smart for violent monsters, are you?" she taunted.

That was it, that got their attention.

"Hey, its that Sturgy girl! exclaimed Leone.

"Get her!"

As soon as Sturgy heard these words she turned around and swam for her life.

She swam past rocky cliffs, neighborhoods and restaurants, but she didn't care. All she cared about was what she was thinking,

(I have to go faster, I have to go faster.)

Just then Sturgy felt something sharp tugging against her tail, it felt like biting. She would feel it for a second and then it would stop, and then continue.

The eels were after her!

(Is this the end of me?) she thought.

THE LONG AND DARING JOURNEY

CHAPTER 11

THE ESCAPE TO THE SPAWNING GROUNDS

The sharp biting that Sturgy had felt on her tail now seemed to be up by her back fins.

(Where's a place to escape?) she wondered frantically.

Then she saw a boat off in the distance.

In big red letters were the words.

EEL FISHING

As Sturgy got closer she saw a gigantic net being pulled out of the water.

"That's it." shouted Sturgy as she began to think up her plan.

(If I can swim fast enough I will swim directly to the net and then with a quick flip of my tail duck down below it. Hopefully Leone and Lee will go plunging into the net just as it is pulled up.)

With all the speed in her body she swam to the net as fast as she could, and just as she was about to hit the net she dove down below it. With a hard flip and swoosh of her tail she escaped the eels and the net.

"Woooooo." came the eels voices from behind her just before they were pulled out of the water in the net.

Sturgy smiled to herself and turned around to go back to the path. When she turned around, a surprising sight greeted her eyes. There rushing towards her were Stephanie, in the lead, and Annie, Cathy, and finally Patty, taking up the back.

"What are you……." started Sturgy before she was knocked over by a gigantic hug.
"Are you okay?" asked Stephanie.
"Yes fine." answered Sturgy.
"But I'm really curious how you all got here," she said.
"Well, as soon as those nasty eels went after you, we followed," answered Annie.
"As simple as that." She added.
"Well." said Sturgy.
"I'm ready to go to the spawning grounds."

The group of 5 Sturgeon swam off together with anticipation and an even greater purpose.

When they finally got to the spawning grounds, the girls all found places that they liked. Spots along the rocks, in the sand and gravel, by the weeds, around fallen trees and rip-rap. Each one found their own special spot and laid their eggs.

That's the story of The Long and Daring Journey.
Thank you for going on this journey with us.

What happened to the first group of fish, you ask?

Well, after the long and daring journey, when she was living in her home, Sturgy received a copy of news coral with a headline that read;

She figured that the group that was captured was the one that had ditched her.

You may also be wondering when did Sturgy help Mr. Crawdad.

Well that's a different story, and you will just have to be patient and wait for it.

Okay, I had better get going on my own journey. I have so much to do to prepare.

Well, goodbye.

Oh, I almost forgot:

The End

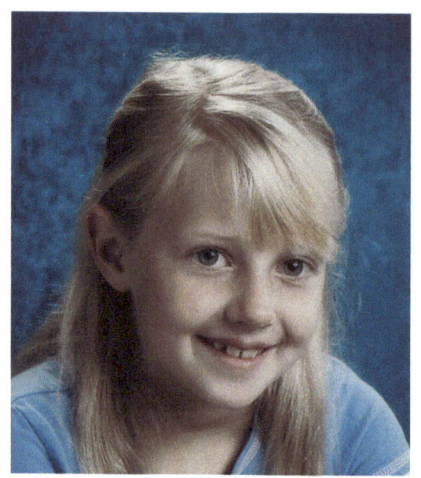

Shenna McLaughlin is an avid Writer,
Storyteller, and Artist from Southern Oregon.

She wrote this Book in 2008 when she
Was 9 years old and a 3ʳᵈ Grade Student.

Writing, and Illustrating since she was 3 years old,,
Shenna has a wonderful imagination and a
Great future ahead of her.

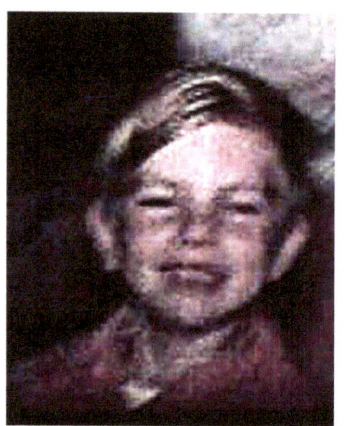

G.R.Fitch is a Sturgeon Artist, Angler,
And Naturalist from Portland, Oregon.
He is the founder of:
The Sturgeon Awareness Foundation
And
The Sturgeon Seekers

For more information on this book or Sturgeon in general
Please check out The Sturgeon Seekers.
http://thesturgeonseekers.tripod.com
Or E-mail
gm.sturg@gmail.com

www.ingramcontent.com/pod-product-compliance
Lightning Source LLC
Chambersburg PA
CBHW041503280526
45792CB00004B/1110